TAUNTON WEST

ROGER SIVITER ARPS

Front cover: On Friday 29 July 1983, Class 47/4 No 47466 approaches Taunton station with the 11.38 Penzance to Manchester train.

The impressive looking signal gantry dominates the scene, and beyond that can be seen the famous 'Forty Steps' footbridge, which completely spans the lines, from where over the years many thousands of pictures have been taken. *Christina Siviter*

Back cover: A busy scene just north of Par station, on the evening of Friday 31 May 1985. On the left hand side, Class 37s Nos 37181 and 37193 with a load of tented china clay wagons move from the down line to the up line to gain access to St Blazey yard, whilst on the right hand siding, Class 37 No 37247 has just stabled a train of clay wagons for the night. Note the words 'Cornish Railways' on the sides of No 37181 and No 37247. *Roger Siviter*

Right: Peak Class 45/1 No 45145 gets the 'right-away' to pull out of Taunton station with a relief afternoon Wolverhampton to Newton Abbot train. 29 July 1983. *Roger Siviter*

© Roger Siviter 2004
Published by Great Bear Publishing
34 Shannon Way, Evesham WR11 3FF Tel: 01386 765134
ISBN 0-9541150-3-1

Designed and produced by Viners Wood Associates Tel: 01452 812813
Printed in England by Ian Allan Printing Ltd, KT12 4RG Tel: 01932 266600

These next two pictures were both taken from 'Forty Steps' footbridge at the western end of Taunton station.

The first scene (above) was taken just after 8 p.m. on Friday 6 July 1984, and shows English Electric Class 50 No 50006 *Neptune* pulling away from Taunton with the (FO) 17.47 Paddington to Plymouth train. At the rear of the train is Taunton West signal box, and on the right hand side can be seen the station avoiding lines for goods traffic. A Class 47 is stabled roughly on the site of the old locomotive shed (83B) which closed in 1964. The late evening midsummer sunshine illuminates the whole scene.

This second view (opposite) shows a Class 31 No 31259 reversing an empty stock train (ECS) into Taunton station (probably the 17.40 to Bristol) on 29 July 1983. At the rear of the train is an unidentified Class 45 locomotive on standby duty. With resignalling in 1986, scenes like this are now but a memory.

Above: *Christina Siviter*; opposite: *Roger Siviter*

Introduction

This book is the fourth volume in the Great Bear Yesteryear Traction series. It complements our first volume '50s WEST' with many different locations, but with a few of the old favourite scenes, which no book on the South-West could arguably be without.

We start our journey at the old county town of Taunton, when the station abounded in splendid GWR signals and signal boxes. We then run through Somerset and cross into Devon at Whiteball, and then on to Exeter, calling at many locations on the way. Between Exeter and Plymouth, the line is covered in detail, and also the Heathfield and Paignton branches. We then travel between Plymouth and Penzance, calling at many of the branch lines. The period covered is from the mid 1970s until the 1990s, the heyday of many of the Classes featured in the book.

In compiling this book, I am grateful to many people, not least the railwaymen who make it all possible, the photographers Hugh Ballantyne, Peter Doel, Peter Gray and Tom Heavyside, and my wife Christina for the typing and, as can be seen, who is also very handy with the camera.

Roger Siviter, Evesham, 2004

BIBLIOGRAPHY

Diesels in the Duchy by John Vaughan
  Published by Ian Allan

Past and Present No 8 Devon by David Mitchell
  Published by Past and Present Publishing

Past and Present No 17 Cornwall by David Mitchell
  Published by Past and Present Publishing

Past and Present No 30 Somerset by David Mitchell
  Published by Past and Present Publishing

50s in Devon and Cornwall by Roger Siviter
  Published by Kingfisher/Runpast Publishing

Above: Prior to re-signalling in the area, Class 08 shunter No 08839 passes Silk Mill Crossing signal box, some two miles west of Taunton station, with an up trip working from Taunton Cider factory on 11 April 1986. Just off the left of the picture is the junction for the cider factory siding, which also forms the connection for the West Somerset Railway which runs on to Minehead. This area is known as Norton Fitzwarren. The signal box closed in 1987.

Hugh Ballantyne

Opposite: Class 47 No 47004 with the 21.58 Stirling to Newton Abbot motorail train leaves the Somerset market town of Wellington behind as it climbs the steep grade of Wellington bank (1 in 86/90) up to Whiteball summit, on 19 May 1979.

Hugh Ballantyne

Left: Just before Whiteball summit is reached, the former GWR main line to Exeter runs through Whiteball tunnel, where it crosses the Somerset/Devon border.

Emerging from Whiteball tunnel (1088 yards long) into the Devonshire sunshine on 5 April 1985 is Class 50 No 50030 *Repulse* with the 09.00 relief Birmingham New Street to Paignton train. The signal box, which dates from the 1950s, semaphore signals and refuge siding would soon all disappear with re-signalling.

On an historical note, the main line from Taunton to Exeter (part of the Bristol & Exeter Railway) was completed in 1844.   *Christina Siviter*

Opposite: A very pleasant autumn scene, taken on 29 October 1980, shows Class 33 No 33015 heading down the 1 in 115 of Whiteball bank towards Burlescombe. The train is a Fawley to Tiverton Junction oil tank train. At the rear of the train can be seen the farm occupation bridge from which the previous picture was taken, under which can be seen Whiteball signal box. Note also, on the right hand side, the siding which has now been removed.   *Tom Heavyside*

Until they started to be withdrawn around 1986, the Class 45, or 'Peak' Class, diesels were regular visitors to the South West. No 45058 is seen here on 19 May 1979 climbing up to Whiteball summit with the 09.20 Paignton to Derby train.

This popular Class of Type 4 diesel locomotive was built by BR at its Crewe and Derby works between 1960 and 1962. The name 'Peak' was derived from the fact that the first eight locomotives were originally named after mountains in the Peak District.   *Hugh Ballantyne*

This picture was taken from the road overbridge seen in the previous photograph, and shows blue liveried Class 47/7 No 47589 heading up Whiteball bank with the 13.00 Plymouth to Paddington train on Friday 5 April 1985.

The use of the telephoto lens highlights the village of Burlescombe and neighbouring quarry. GWR semaphore signals complete this springtime scene.   *Roger Siviter*

Our next location is Tiverton Junction, one-time junction for the lines to Hemyock, to the east, and Tiverton, to the west, the latter closing in 1964 and the former surviving until October 1975, albeit from 1963 for milk traffic only.

Class 45 No 45050 speeds through Tiverton Junction on Tuesday 24 July 1984 with the late-running 09.22 Newcastle to Penzance train. Note the fine array of GWR signals and the signal box on the up platform.

This station closed on 9 May 1986 and was replaced by Tiverton Parkway station, which opened on 12 May 1986. The new station is situated a mile or so north of the old junction station, which was finally demolished in the early 1990s.

A visit to this location now would show few visible signs of there having once been a busy junction station.   *Christina Siviter*

Opposite: The pleasant Devon countryside a mile or so south west of Tiverton Junction is our next scene, as on the evening of Sunday 19 August 1984 Class 50 No 50007 *Sir Edward Elgar* heads north eastwards with the 17.45 Plymouth to Bristol train.

No 50007 was originally named *Hercules* but was re-named and re-furbished in GWR green in the early 1980s, *Sir Edward Elgar* having been a member of the famous Castle Class – No 7005 – hence the cast number plate. Since withdrawal, it has been preserved by the 'Class 40 Appeal'. Beyond the fence on the left hand side is the M5 motorway.

Roger Siviter

Right: On the early evening of Monday 7 May 1985 (May Day) a nicely lined out Class 45 No 45013 approaches the old Devon market town of Cullompton with a St Blazey to Severn Tunnel Junction freight train.

Behind the photographer is the site of Cullompton station, which closed in 1964. Where the down station building, goods shed and small goods yard once stood is now an M5 motorway service station.

On the left of our picture is the motorway, but this is completely obscured by a fine avenue of trees. Mind you, having experienced the bottlenecks and jams on the old A38 through Cullompton in the late 1940s and 1950s, I should imagine many residents welcomed the coming of the M5 in the late 1960s.

Christina Siviter

Above: With a timely burst of spring sunshine, the 08.55 Penzance to Newcastle train speeds through Hele & Bradninch (some nine miles north of Exeter) hauled by Class 45/1 No 45120, on 28 May 1985.

The semaphore signalling was destined to survive until 9 December 1985, when control of this area was taken over by the new power box at Exeter St Davids station.   *Christina Siviter*

Opposite: A very pleasant location from which to photograph up trains is just north of the village of Rewe, some five miles north of Exeter. Brush Class 47/8 No 47845 *County of Kent* in Virgin red livery, complete with a rake of red-liveried carriages, looks a treat in the early autumn sunshine as it heads towards Taunton with the 10.40 Plymouth to Birmingham New Street train. In the background is the village of Rewe. 8 October 1998.   *Roger Siviter*

Above: Cowley Bridge, the junction of the Paddington line with the former SR line to Barnstaple and Okehampton, is no doubt a familiar location to many readers, but a Class 58 locomotive working through there is arguably a fairly rare occurrence. When I lived at Exmouth in 1998, during the summer months, especially in June and July with the long evening sunshine, I was able to pop out and photograph a good amount of early evening freight traffic, plus the locomotive-hauled passenger trains. And so on the evening of Friday 30 July 1998 at Cowley Bridge junction, I was more than a little surprised and pleased to photograph Class 58 No 58026 (in Railfreight grey) on the 13.07 Whatley to Exeter Riverside stone train (head code 7285) which was normally worked by a pair of Class 37 locomotives. The last time I had seen a Class 58 in Devon was on 1 September 1984 at Aller junction, when *(continued opposite)*

(cont) No 58002 appeared in charge of the 12.10 Liverpool to Plymouth HST service, the Class 58 having been put on the failed HST unit at Birmingham New Street. A memorable occasion! The 3300hp Class 58s were built by BREL at Doncaster Works during 1983 to 1987, and are now more or less withdrawn, having been replaced by the Class 66 locomotives, which were built in Canada and introduced in the late 1990s.

Roger Siviter

Above: Turning round from the previous picture, and a few days earlier on the afternoon of 27 July 1998, we see a brace of English Electric Class 37s, Nos 37010 and 37047, as they leave Exeter Riverside yard and head for the Westbury area with a train of empty stone box wagons. The locomotive liveries are worth noting, No 37010 in the yellow and grey 'Dutch' livery and No 37047 in Mainline blue.

Roger Siviter

Class 25 No 25080 and Class 50 No 50042 (which had failed earlier) enter Exeter St Davids station on 15 June 1974 with the 13.30 Paddington to Penzance train, which by this time was running approximately 100 minutes late. The Class 25 Type 2 locomotives were built by BR at their Crewe, Darlington and Derby works.

They were first introduced in 1961, and were an up-rated version of the Class 24s, which came into service in 1957. They worked in the south west for around a decade from the early 1970s. They were withdrawn from service on BR in the mid-1980s. However, several examples remain in preservation. *Peter Gray*

Conversation piece at Exeter St Davids station on Tuesday 28 August 1984, as Class 47 No 47324 waits to leave the centre road with a down ECS train bound for Plymouth. In the middle distance can be seen Exeter West signal box which, together with the gantry and other signals, would disappear in the following year with the opening of Exeter power box. This signal box is preserved at Crewe Heritage Centre. The lines swinging away to the left of the locomotive are the former SR route to Exeter Central station, and then on to Salisbury and Waterloo.

Roger Siviter

Above: Super power is provided by a pair of Class 33 'Crompton' Type 3 locomotives, Nos 33113 and 33014. The pair are seen reversing a three-coach ECS train into platform 3 at Exeter St Davids on Saturday 7 July 1984. Once in the platform, the ECS train will be attached to the coaching stock that is already there, which will then form the 16.18 service to Waterloo, to be hauled by the Class 33s. Overlooking the scene is a splendid example of a GWR bracket signal.

Christina Siviter

Opposite: On 19 August 1989, Class 47 No 47500 *Great Western* passes the former GWR signal box (now a tool store) and the site of Exminster station with the 14.58 Penzance to Milton Keynes train. No 47500 is in GWR livery, complete with cast name plate. Several of this Class were turned out in this livery in 1985 to celebrate the 'GWR 150' year, including No 47484 *Isambard Kingdom Brunel*. Exminster station closed in 1964, and the signal box in 1986.

Hugh Ballantyne

Opposite: After Exminster, the line for several miles follows the estuary of the River Exe, as can well be seen in this next picture.

On the evening of 24 August 1998, a pair of Class 37/5s Nos 37670 and 37674, in smart red and grey liveries respectively, are caught by the camera near Starcross with the 08.57 Cliffe Vale (Stoke on Trent) to St Blazey (Par) china clay empties, which runs on Mondays, Wednesdays and Fridays only.

1998 was more or less the Indian Summer for the Class 37s in the South-West. By the following year, most of their duties had been taken over by the Class 66s.   *Roger Siviter*

Right above: An immaculate Class 33 No 33051 crosses the causeway at Cockwood Harbour on Tuesday evening 25 August 1987 with the 16.40 Paignton to Exeter train.

These attractive Type 3 locomotives were first introduced in 1960 and built by the Birmingham Railway Carriage & Wagon Company, Smethwick. The nickname 'Cromptons' derives from their traction motors being manufactured by Crompton Parkinson. With a tractive effort of 45000lb and a maximum speed of 85mph, they were suitable for a wide range of work. Although most of the Class have been withdrawn, a few locomotives still remain, and are now chiefly used on special charter trains.   *Roger Siviter*

Right below: An earlier picture at Cockwood, taken on an August evening in 1976, shows a Type 2 Class 25 No 25080 hurrying along the causeway with an Exeter to Paignton train. These locomotives lasted in the area until around 1981, when many of their duties were taken over by Class 31 and Class 33 locomotives.   *Peter Doel*

Opposite: At around 09.00 a.m. on Sunday 8 July 1984, an immaculate looking Class 45 No 45069 trundles through Dawlish Warren station with a ballast/track maintenance train – a somewhat unusual and lowly task for a Type 4 locomotive. Although semaphore signals still seem to abound in this picture, there are already signs of re-signalling about to take place. *Christina Siviter*

Right: On summer Saturdays in the late 1980s, several holiday trains from the North-West to Paignton were hauled by pairs of Brush Class 31 locomotives. These included the 09.18 Manchester–Paignton and the 09.33 Stockport–Paignton.

On 2 September 1989, the train from Manchester, hauled by Nos 31432 and 31452, is seen travelling through Dawlish Warren, and heading towards Dawlish and Teignmouth. This picture was taken from Langstone Rock, a popular spot with photographers.

The Type 2 Class 31s were built between 1957 and 1962 by Brush Traction at Loughborough. No 31432 and No 31452 are actually Class 31/4s, having been modified in the early 1980s from the earlier design.

Roger Siviter

Opposite: With Langstone Rock in the right hand background, Class 50 No 50048 *Dauntless* runs along the sea wall to Dawlish with the all-stations (except Torre) 11.30 Exeter to Paignton train, on Sunday 23 August 1987. The famous red cliffs compliment the Network South-East livery of the locomotive.

These powerful Type 4 locomotives were built during 1967–1968 by the English Electric Co. at Vulcan Foundry, Newton le Willows. They first appeared in the South West in the mid 1970s with the demise of the famous Western Hydraulic locomotives.

Roger Siviter

Above: This panoramic view of Dawlish was taken from the cliff top park known as Early's Wall on the south west side of this famous Devon seaside resort.

On 30 July 1998, Class 47 No 47742 has just run through Dawlish station and is heading towards Teignmouth with the 12.18 Bristol to Plymouth mail van train. The station can be seen on the right hand side, and running by the side of the track is Marine Parade, where the hotels and flats, etc. have a splendid view out to sea as well as, of course, the former GWR main line. *Roger Siviter*

Shell, or Horse, Cove is our next picture, famous in GWR days as the setting for publicity posters. With the tide nicely in, and Dawlish in the background, Class 31/4 No 31419 runs through this picturesque location with the 13.20 Exeter to Paignton stopping train, on Thursday 20 August 1987, 50 minutes being allowed for the 28 mile journey, including nine stops. *Roger Siviter*

The last of the tunnels, running westwards, between Dawlish and Teignmouth (some four miles apart) is the well-known Parson & Clerk tunnel, a mile or so from Teignmouth station. This striking picture, taken from not the usual angle, shows Class 46 No 46018 emerging from Parson & Clerk tunnel on 17 August 1979 with a down mixed goods train. The line is just crossing over an inlet of the sea and also the end of Smugglers Lane, which leads to the sea wall promenade. Note also the PW hut on the left hand side. *Hugh Ballantyne*

Above: Class 47 No 47091 runs along the sea wall at Teignmouth with the Paddington to St Austell motorail train on Saturday 7 July 1984. Prior to 1982, the train ran from Kensington with provision for passengers to travel on carriages attached to the train. However, from 1982 the train left from Paddington, with passengers travelling separately by the normal HST service.

At St Austell, by the summer service of 1984, the sidings which had originally been used by the motorail passenger carriages had been removed. This area was then turned into a car park, leaving only one siding for the bogie wagons, plus a short spur line.

Christina Siviter

Opposite: The classic scene at Teignmouth, on 12 April 1983, as Class 45/1 No 45122 passes under the famous skew-bridge with the morning Plymouth to Manchester train.

Above the train and under the bridge is the United Reform church, and on the left hand side is St. Michael's church, complete with the flag of St. George.

Christina Siviter

Opposite: These next two pictures were taken from the road/pedestrian bridge, seen just beyond the skew-bridge in the previous picture.

Framed by the skew-bridge, Class 47 No 47703, in Fragonset black livery, heads inland towards Teignmouth station with the 10.17 Manchester to Penzance service on 15 August 1998. In the far background can be seen Sandy Bay, which is situated between the east Devon seaside resorts of Exmouth and Budleigh Salterton.

The second picture (looking the other way) was taken some years earlier, on 7 July 1984, and shows Class 47/3 No 47311 'clagging' well as it pulls away from Teignmouth station with the 10.20 Paignton to Edinburgh/Glasgow train. Just to the right of the train under the attractive road bridge can be seen a GWR semaphore signal, which by the following year with re-signalling would disappear.
Left: Roger Siviter. Right: Christina Siviter

Above: On 17 August 1979, Class 46 No 46007 approaches Shaldon bridge on the outskirts of Teignmouth with the 10.23 Manchester to Plymouth service. On the right hand side can be seen the edge of Teignmouth dockyard. From here to Newton Abbot, a distance of around five miles, the line follows the estuary of the River Teign.

The Class 46s, which were a development of the 'Peak' (45) Class, were first introduced in 1961. They had all been withdrawn by the mid 1980s, but examples remain in preservation.
Hugh Ballantyne

Newly refurbished Class 50 No 50047 *Swiftsure* runs down by the side of the Teign estuary towards Teignmouth with the 07.40 Penzance to Birmingham train on 12 April 1983.

All the Class 50s were refurbished by the early 1980s, most being turned out in the 'large logo' livery. However, as can be seen, certain of the Class were repainted in the old BR blue livery. By 1992, the Class had been withdrawn, with No 50047 having been an early casualty, being taken out in April 1988.

Happily, many of the Class have been preserved, and can be seen at work on main line charters, as well as the Heritage lines such as the Severn Valley Railway. There are also two societies – the '50 Fund' and the 'Class 50 Society' – which are actively engaged in the preservation of these popular locomotives. *Christina Siviter*

A fairly rare occurrence in the South West, on Sunday 28 May 1984, when a pair of English Electric Class 40s, Nos 40057 and 40135, ran from Preston to Paignton with a special charter train – 'The Devonian'. Having worked to Paignton, the pair of 'Whistlers' with No 40135 leading then ran light engine to Exeter for refuelling, and are seen here having just passed under the signal gantry at the east end of Newton Abbot station, en route to Exeter.

These attractive looking locomotives were amongst the earliest Type 4 diesel locomotives on BR, being introduced in 1958. They were withdrawn by the mid-1980s, but several examples have been preserved and can be seen at work on main line charter trains.

Note the GWR signal box, just to the left of which is the line to Heathfield, the subject of our next two pictures. *Christina Siviter*

The line from Newton Abbot to Heathfield (now freight only) was part of the Teign Valley line to Exeter. The branch line to Mortonhampstead also ran from Heathfield, but this line closed completely in 1964, by which time so had the Teign Valley line. The Heathfield line was kept open to service the oil terminal at Heathfield and also a clay works, as well as Newton Abbot Clays (an offshoot of English China Clays) situated just north of Newton Abbot.

On a true winter's day in February 1985 (a rarity in Devon) an unidentified Class 31 is seen shunting in the siding for Newton Abbot Clays. Note the tented wagon in the foreground. *Peter Doel*

Class 33 No 33162 is pictured on the Heathfield branch at Teign Bridge in September 1985 with a return trip working from Heathfield to Exeter. In the background are the old-style crossing gates, a notable feature on this line. Also above the trees in the middle background can be seen the hills of Dartmoor National Park. Also worthy of note is the early model Land Rover with its distinctive inset headlamps.

Peter Doel

The South Devon Railway from Exeter reached the market town of Newton Abbot in 1846, from when it became an important railway town, complete with locomotive shed and works. Although by 1983 when this next picture was taken the works and depot had closed, there was much that still denoted a busy junction station.

This view, taken on the afternoon of 30 July 1983 of Class 45 No 45059 leaving the station with the 08.26 Bradford to Paignton train, shows much infrastructure from the past, including many attractive semaphore signals and

signal box, also a very spacious GWR station with fine platform canopies, plus several through routes and freight sidings – note the line of tented clay wagons. In the background on the right hand side is the diesel depot which was built on the site of the old steam shed (83A) and on the extreme right are the offices of the publishers David & Charles, which used to be the wagon works. By 1987, with re-signalling in the area, this scene would change drastically, with all the sidings, etc. being taken up, leaving just three lines through the station.

Roger Siviter

Above: Class 47/4 No 47444 *University of Nottingham* glows in the evening sunshine as it climbs up to Aller junction with a Plymouth bound train of empty ballast wagons on 22 April 1987.

The Type 4 Class 47 locomotives were built either by Brush Traction at Loughborough or by BR at their Crewe works. They were introduced in 1962, and over the years have seen many modifications, etc. as well as being turned out in a variety of liveries including, as seen here, the popular 'large logo' livery, complete with silver roof.

Note also the elegant signal gantry which, within a few days of this picture being taken, would be replaced by colour light signalling.   *Roger Siviter*

Opposite: A fine summer's evening at Aller junction, as Class 45/1 No 45110 runs downgrade towards Newton Abbot with the 16.00 Penzance to Derby train on 31 August 1985.

There is much to enjoy in this pastoral scene, not least of all, the junction signal box complete with a well-tended allotment. At the rear of the train can be seen the Paignton line going straight ahead, and the Plymouth line swinging away to the right (up Dainton bank) towards Totnes.

Within two years with re-signalling, Aller would be a junction no more, with the two sets of lines now diverging.   *Christina Siviter*

Opposite: The branch line to Paignton opened in 1859. Originally it ran to Kingswear, but this section was sold by BR in 1972 to the Dart Valley Railway Co. This is now known as the Paignton & Dartmouth Railway, and is very popular with enthusiasts and the many visitors that holiday in the Torbay area.

A unique occasion on 2 May 1994, as a triple-header of English Electric Type 3 Class 37 diesels Nos 37799, 37796 and 37896 climb out of Torre station (just north of Torquay) with the 17.32 ECS working from Goodrington carriage sidings to Exeter. Once at Exeter, the ECS will then form a special charter train to Paddington.   *Hugh Ballantyne*

Right: Summer Saturdays on the Paignton branch are obviously busy with many (Saturdays only) holiday trains from all over the country.

On Saturday 18 August 1984, Class 50 No 50016 *Barham* speeds along between Kingkerswell and Torre with the 08.15 Cardiff to Paignton train, just one of the many summer Saturday trains running down to Torquay and Paignton on that sunny day.   *Christina Siviter*

We are now back on the main line to Plymouth, overlooking the western side of Dainton bank. This picture was taken from the hill by the entrance to Dainton tunnel, and shows Class 50 No 50026 *Indomitable* as it climbs the 1 in 37 up to the tunnel with the 10.27 Penzance to Edinburgh/Glasgow train on 23 April 1987.

Notice the utilitarian looking signal box and also, on either side of the main line, the track beds of the relief sidings, which give a good idea of the steepness of the western side of the bank.

Roger Siviter

On a cold but sunny 22 December 1987, one of Plymouth Laira's Class 37/5s No 37674 hurries through Totnes station with a mid morning down mixed goods, bound for Plymouth Tavistock junction yard, and probably on to St Blazey. Although Totnes was re-signalled in 1985, the by-now redundant signal box looks in good order. Later on, this box after use as a store was turned into the excellent 'Signal Box Cafe' which not only serves the station but also the adjacent creamery. In the bottom right of the picture can also be seen a trio of luggage trolleys, probably dating from GWR days. *Roger Siviter*

On leaving Totnes station, down trains face the five miles of Rattery bank, which at its steepest is 1 in 47. No problems however for the 12.18 Bristol to Plymouth mail van train as it starts the climb out of Totnes on 24 August 1998, double headed by Class 47s Nos 47793 *St Augustine* and 47789, both in Parcels Sector red livery.

Roger Siviter

Brent, the former junction station for the branch line to Kingsbridge (which closed in 1963), closed in 1964, but as a reminder of past days, the old signal box still remains today, albeit now used as a tool store, and also the old goods shed, now in commercial use. With the hills of Dartmoor National Park in the background and the mid-winter sun illuminating the scene, Class 47 No 47005 heads through the site of Brent station on 16 January 1988 with the 14.15 Plymouth to Leeds van train. On the left hand side is the attractive looking former signal box. Off the left hand side is the old goods shed. *Christina Siviter*

Opposite: For ten of the next fifteen miles to Plymouth, the line hugs the edge of Dartmoor National Park. The principal Dartmoor town on this section is Ivybridge, which lies at the foot of Harford Moor. At Dinnaton, just west of Ivybridge, on 23 April 1988, a pair of Class 37/5 locomotives No 37675 *William Cookworthy* and No 37673 (both in the attractive Railfreight livery) head towards Exeter with the 14.55 St Blazey to Gloucester goods train. In the distant background can be seen the china clay workings at Crownhill Down. *Roger Siviter*

Above: In beautiful evening sunshine, Class 47/3 No 47315 leaves Mutley tunnel and approaches Plymouth North Road station with a down tank train, on 28 May 1985.

Above the entrance to the tunnel is now a multi-storey car park. Note also the fine row of Edwardian terrace houses. Although less than half a mile from North Road station, Mutley once boasted a small station, which closed in the 1960s. *Christina Siviter*

Carefully observing the 15mph speed limit, Class 47/8 No 47847 heads off the Royal Albert Bridge into Cornwall, and approaches Saltash station with the 08.40 Glasgow to Penzance train on the evening of Wednesday 19 August 1998.

This famous rail bridge was built by Isambard Kingdom Brunel in 1859, and the Tamar road bridge was completed in 1961.

Roger Siviter

Just to the west of Saltash station is Coombe viaduct, which crosses over a tributary inlet of the River Tamar.

The unusual combination of Class 37 No 37118 and Class 45 No 45006 *Honourable Artillery Company* make a fine sight as they head across Coombe viaduct on the evening of 17 August 1984 with the 14.45 St Blazey to Severn Tunnel Junction goods train. This photograph was taken from the edge of the small goods yard which served Saltash station, which is now a private estate of luxury flats.

Christina Siviter

Opposite: The old GWR Cornish main line possesses many fine viaducts, but amongst the most impressive must be Lynher viaduct, situated some four miles west of Saltash.

On 1 September 1993, Class 47/4 No 47474 *Sir Rowland Hill* crosses over the elegant eight-arch viaduct with the 12.18 Penzance to Paddington parcels train. Enthusiasts will no doubt notice the palindromic symmetry of the locomotive's number! The name of the locomotive is also of interest, as Sir Rowland Hill (who was born in Kidderminster) was the inventor of the 'Penny Post'.   *Roger Siviter*

Right: Class 47/4 No 47538 in blue livery makes a contrast with the rake of mainly InterCity liveried coaches, which together form the 10.27 Penzance to Edinburgh and Glasgow service. The train will split at Carstairs Junction, just over twenty miles from both Scottish cities. Arrival in Edinburgh is scheduled for 22.24, and at Glasgow Central by 22.23, a journey of just under six hours for around six hundred miles.

The location of this picture, which was taken on 5 May 1988, is near Menheniot. At the rear of the train can be seen Tresulgan viaduct, which was originally one of Brunel's timber viaducts, having been rebuilt in brick in 1899.   *Roger Siviter*

Above: On 27 August 1987, Class 37/5 No 37675 is seen heading through Coombe Junction halt with a china clay train from Moorswater to Liskeard. At the rear of the train can be seen one of the arches of Moorswater viaduct, which carries the Cornish main line.

The junction for the line to Liskeard and the line to Looe are at the rear of the photographer. *Roger Siviter*

Opposite: The following day (28 August 1987) another Class 37/4 locomotive, this time No 37672, with a clay train from Moorswater, climbs towards Liskeard where it will gain the Plymouth to Penzance main line, seen in the background crossing over Liskeard viaduct. The line from Liskeard to Moorswater is also part of the branch line to the popular holiday and fishing village of Looe. Trains for Looe reverse at Coombe Junction halt (see previous picture). *Roger Siviter*

Opposite: Class 37/5 No 37521 is just entering the old GWR station at Liskeard on the afternoon of 12 April 1994 with a train of china clay tank wagons from Moorswater, bound for Lostwithiel. Note the train is on the up line, but will gain the down line at the crossover points, just to the west of the station.

Worthy of note are the signal box and fine array of GWR semaphore signals, including the centre-balanced signal just above the left of the train. The platform for the Looe branch is just out of sight at the rear of the train. Sadly, the bracket signal by the crossover at the eastern end of the station has been replaced by a colour light signal. *Roger Siviter*

Right: There are several viaducts between Doublebois and Bodmin Parkway station (formerly Bodmin Road) where the line runs through the Fowey or Glynn Valley and follows the course of the River Fowey.

On Saturday 1 June 1985, an unidentified Class 47 locomotive (believed to be No 47472) heads across Pendalake viaduct with the 08.50 Newquay to Manchester train. In the background can be seen the southern edge of Bodmin Moor. Pendalake viaduct is situated around two miles east of Bodmin Parkway station. *Christina Siviter*

Left above: Class 45/1 No 45143 *5th Royal Inniskilling Dragoon Guards* slows down as it enters Bodmin Parkway station where it will stop with the 07.50 Bristol to Penzance train on 30 May 1984.

The station was the junction for the GWR line to Bodmin and Boscarne junction, where it connected with the LSWR lines to Wenford and Wadebridge (see next picture below)

On the left of the picture can be seen the line which leads to Bodmin General station. After closure, this line was preserved and is now known as the Bodmin & Wenford Railway.   *Christina Siviter*

Left below: Traffic on the Wenfordbridge line (from Bodmin Road via Boscarne junction) ended on 26 September 1983.

On 19 November 1980, Class 08 No 08113 ambles down the densely wooded Wenfordbridge branch, which follows the valley of the River Camel, with clay wagons bound for Bodmin Road and Lostwithiel (for Carne Point on the Fowey branch).

The English Electric Class 08 shunting locomotives were built between 1952 and 1962, and although many have been withdrawn from service, some can still be seen at work on the British railway system. Several examples have been preserved, but a number are now in private use in industrial locations.   *Hugh Ballantyne*

Opposite: We are now back on the Plymouth –Penzance main line at Newton, between Bodmin Parkway and Lostwithiel, as a smart looking Class 47/5 No 47592 *County of Avon* climbs the 1 in 65 up to Bodmin Parkway with a north bound mineral train at mid morning on 15 February 1988.

They say that spring often arrives early in Cornwall and perhaps this picture well proves that point.   *Roger Siviter*

Opposite: During the winter timetable of 1993/94, there was an overnight parcels train from Leeds to Penzance, which departed from Leeds at 21.52 and arrived at Penzance at around 10.00 the following morning. This meant that it ran through the Lostwithiel area between 08.30 and 09.00.

In pleasant sunshine, Class 47 No 47762 approaches Lostwithiel with the eight van parcels train from Leeds on the morning of Wednesday 13 April 1994. In the background can be seen part of the ruins of Restormel Castle, which dates from mediaeval times. Note the sidings often used to store clay wagons.
Roger Siviter

Above: On the evening of 27 April 1984, Class 37 No 37207 plus goods van runs over the crossing at the eastern end of Lostwithiel station and heads westwards towards Par and St Blazey yard. The locomotive, which is named *William Cookworthy*, is finished in the distinctive Cornish Railways livery, complete with the Cornish flag and BR logo, etc. on the front end, and the Cornish lizard on the side of the locomotive. Framing this short but smart looking train is the attractive GWR signal box, and on the up platform, a GWR-type semaphore signal.

Lostwithiel is also the junction for the line to Carne Point on the old Fowey branch, from where the china clay is shipped. Just to the right of the signal box can be seen the end of the sidings where the china clay trains for Carne Point are shunted and assembled. Passenger traffic to Fowey ceased on 4 January 1965.
Roger Siviter

Opposite: Although the Fowey branch lost its passenger traffic in 1965, the following years have seen a continual procession of clay trains to the docks at Carne Point, which is situated just north of the now demolished station at Fowey.

The branch runs along the side of the River Fowey, and at Golant it runs on a causeway across the attractive little harbour. This picture was taken from the hillside to the south of the harbour on the afternoon of 15 February 1988, and shows Class 37/5 No 37673 heading for Carne Point with a train of china clay. From Carne Point, the china clay is shipped world wide. *Roger Siviter*

Right: From the hillside just to the south of Lostwithiel station, you get an almost aerial view of the railway and much of the surrounding valley.

Class 37 No 37254 in the distinctive 'Dutch' livery has just left Lostwithiel station area, and is beginning the steep climb up to Treverrin tunnel (1 in 57 at its steepest) with a train of empty clay wagons, which it had earlier brought up from Carne Point. At this spot the train has just crossed over the River Fowey, and just beyond the train to the left of the station, the milk depot and creamery is visible. Also, to the right of the locomotive can be seen the start of the Fowey branch. This picture was taken on the evening of 13 April 1994, and shows the station sidings full of clay wagons, no doubt in readiness for the following day's work. *Roger Siviter*

Opposite: In the previous caption, I have mentioned Treverrin tunnel. This scene, taken on 31 May 1985 (by kind permission of BR), shows Class 47/4 No 47540 leaving the western end of the tunnel with the 12.02 Birmingham New Street to Penzance train. The rhododendrons are in full bloom, and complement the locomotive's blue livery, and the evening sun also highlights the typical GWR-style tunnel mouth.   *Roger Siviter*

Right: Just to the north of Par station is the crossover junction for the St Blazey/Newquay line, enabling goods traffic to take the loopline by the side of Par station, which leads on to St Blazey yard and then on to the Newquay branch. This can be especially useful if a Newquay train is in the branch platform, which is platform three.

Class 45 No 45036, with distinctive split headcodes, takes the St Blazey line just north of Par station with a down goods train for St Blazey yard, on 27 April 1984.

To the left of the train can be seen what was once a common sight – a goods van turned into a garden shed.   *Roger Siviter*

The late evening sunshine highlights Class 37 No 37247 as it reverses a train of tented china clay wagons out of Par station into the down siding just beyond the road bridge, on the last day of August 1984. On the right is the former GWR station building, complete with a fine canopy, and in the background overlooking the scene is the Royal Hotel. Also, just visible on the left hand side at the end of the platform are the lines to Newquay and St Blazey.

The English Electric Type 3 Class 37s were built between 1960 and 1965. Over the years (like the Class 47s) several have received modifications, including No 37247, which within a year or so of this picture was refurbished and reclassified as a Class 37/5. It then received the new number 37671, and was appropriately given the Cornish name *Tre Pol and Pen*.   *Roger Siviter*

With the end of the summer timetable on 4 October 1987, scheduled locomotive hauled trains ended on the Newquay branch. At the same time, the trackwork at Newquay station was modified, leaving only a single line in and out of the station, with no run around facilities. And so today, summer Saturday trains from London, Birmingham, etc. are in the hands of HST units.

In the last summer of locomotive hauled trains, Class 50 No 50032 *Courageous* approaches Luxulyan, some four miles from Par, with the 11.10 Paddington to Newquay train. 22 August 1987.   *Roger Siviter*

Opposite: Around eight miles from Newquay is St Dennis junction where, on the evening of 30 May 1984, a three-car Class 118 DMU passes the junction signal box with the 19.55 Par to Newquay service. These units were first introduced in 1960, and built by Birmingham RC&W Co.

The line on the right hand side of the box once ran through to Burngullow on the Plymouth Penzance main line, with the extreme right hand line being the start of the short branch line to Meledor Mill. The line on the extreme left hand side was used on summer Saturdays as a passing loop for the Newquay branch trains, but this disappeared together with the signal box, which closed in 1987.

It should be added here that there is still some clay traffic on the branch between Goonbarrow (just west of Luxulyan) and St Blazey/Par, and on to Carne Point on the Fowey branch.   *Christina Siviter*

Right: We return to the main Plymouth to Penzance route, just one and a half miles west of Par, where the line runs through the exclusive Carlyon Bay golf course, which is situated within a few hundred yards of St Austell Bay.

With the chimneys of the clay drying plant at Par dominating the background, Class 50 No 50012 *Benbow* climbs the steep grade up to Carlyon Bay with the 10.18 Paddington to Penzance train on 31 May 1985.   *Roger Siviter*

An attractive scene at St Austell on an August Saturday in 1974, as a pair of 'Rats' (Class 25s) Nos 25326 and 25275 pull out of the old GWR station with a midday Penzance to Plymouth parcels train (4B17). On the right are the motor rail sidings used by the Kensington to St Austell Motorail service, which until 1982 carried passenger coaches (see picture on page 28).

At the time, this area was controlled by semaphore signalling; the signal box can be seen at the rear of the train. Manual signalling lasted until 1980, with the advent of colour lights.

In the far distance can be seen the china clay (or 'white') mountains around the Burngullow area.

Peter Gray

This picture was taken from the other end of St Austell station, about ten years later on 31 August 1984, and shows Class 37 No 37247 pulling through the station with a load of clay empties bound for the Burngullow area.

There is a car park on the left hand side where the Motorail carriage sidings once were, presumably for the cars that travelled on that service. Normal station parking is on the right hand side of the picture, where there is an excellent selection of cars from the 1970s and early 1980s.

Note also that the GWR station building on the down platform has recently been replaced with a modern construction.

Roger Siviter

Between St Austell and Burngullow, a distance of three miles, the line runs across two handsome viaducts, St Austell and Gover. On Friday 17 August 1984, the 09.40 Paddington to Penzance train crosses over St Austell viaduct, double headed by Class 50s, Nos 50050 *Fearless* and 50027 *Lion*. Arrival in Penzance is scheduled for 15.35, just under six hours for the 305½ mile journey from Paddington, including ten station stops.   *Christina Siviter*

Immaculate Class 37/5 No 37674 slowly approaches Burngullow junction with a train of clay tanks from the clay works at Parkandillack, on 11 April 1988. This branch line, which also serves the china clay mill at Drinnick by means of a reversal at Nandern Wharf, originally ran through to St Dennis junction on the Par to Newquay line, but this was severed at Parkandillack in 1966. (See picture on page 64) The main line from Burngullow to Probus (some seven miles to the west) was singled in 1986, and the signal box on the left hand side was closed at the same time. However, this was used for many years as a tool store.

The station at Burngullow closed in 1931, but this picture shows one of the up platform buildings (opposite the signal box) surviving, as it still does today, albeit now all covered in ivy. Sadly, there is now very little left of the signal box.

Roger Siviter

Above: On 18 September 1981, Class 47 No 47029, having finished its shunting work, heads away from Parkandillack (the end of the china clay branch) with a short freight train for Burngullow, and then on to Par. On the right hand side is the edge of the clay works owned by English China Clays (ECC), and in the background is the village of Hendra.

The line from Burngullow to St Dennis junction was opened in 1869 as part of the Newquay & Cornwall Junction Railway. *Hugh Ballantyne*

Opposite: We leave the Parkandillack branch and return to the Penzance main line, some three miles west of Burngullow at Coombe St Stephen viaduct. Class 45/1 No 45136 hurries over the viaduct at around 8.45 p.m. on the evening of 29 May 1985 with the 09.23 Newcastle to Penzance train.

Most pictures at this attractive viaduct were usually taken from the east side of the tracks, more often than not from the fields at the back of the train. It is only on a mid summer's evening that this picture is really possible. Note also the double track, which was singled as far as Probus in 1986. *Christina Siviter*

Above: For the next nine miles from Coombe St Stephen to Truro, the line runs through pleasant countryside, including the area around Buckshead, some two miles east of Cornwall's only city. On 5 April 1988, Class 50 No 50036 *Victorious* negotiates the reverse curves at Buckshead, and runs down to Truro with the relief train to the 10.50 Paddington to Penzance service. *Roger Siviter*

Opposite: Class 50 No 50050 *Fearless* crosses Carvedras viaduct, just before entering Truro station with the 07.00 Exeter to Penzance train, on 30 May 1985. Below the viaduct lie the Victoria Gardens, and overlooking the scene is the church of St George the Martyr. *Christina Siviter*

Just to the west of Truro station is Penwithers junction, the junction for the 12¼ mile branch line to the port of Falmouth. This line was opened in 1863, and unlike some other branch lines, it still survives today, with a reasonable service.

There are several viaducts on this line, including Carnon viaduct. On 28 April 1983, a three-car Class 118 DMU heads off this viaduct towards Falmouth with the 18.10 service from Truro.
Tom Heavyside

During the nine miles between Truro and the former tin mining town of Redruth, the scenery changes considerably, from rural agricultural land to a mining landscape. This is especially so from Scorrier, just north of Redruth, to Camborne, a distance of around six miles. However, since tin mining has virtually ended in the area, much work has taken place over the last few years, with land reclamation and new roads, etc.

But happily, Redruth still retains its fine looking station, complete with GWR station buildings, canopies and attractive looking footbridge.

Freight traffic is not plentiful to the west of Burngullow, but in the mid 1990s on Tuesdays only, a train of four-wheel fuel oil tanks was run between Tavistock junction (Plymouth) and Ponsandane (Penzance) and return, usually headed by a Class 37 locomotive.

On 3 September 1996, Class 37/5 No 37696 runs through the former GWR station at Redruth with the (TO) 15.30 Tavistock junction to Ponsandane tank train.

Roger Siviter

Earlier I mentioned the mining landscape around Redruth and Camborne, and this next picture, taken on 30 July 1988, well illustrates this. Class 47/4 No 47536 runs through Carn Brea (just to the north of Camborne) with the 10.17 Penzance to Manchester train. Even by this date, the landscape is beginning to change, but note the Cornish engine houses in the background of the picture, a reminder of the industrial past of this former tin mining area.

On the left hand side of the picture, the donkey takes a pause during grazing – perhaps to watch the train go by!

Hugh Ballantyne

Six miles after Camborne, the line runs through the holiday resort of Hayle, some seven miles from Penzance.

On the evening of 30 May 1985, Class 45/1 No 45109 runs over the 227 yard long Hayle viaduct with the 12.02 Birmingham to Penzance train. At this point, the viaduct is crossing over Hayle Harbour, which runs into the River Hayle, which then runs into the famous St Ives Bay. The area around Hayle is the narrowest part of Cornwall, with the distance between the Atlantic Ocean and the English Channel being less than five miles. *Christina Siviter*

Before the line reaches Penzance, it runs through St Erth, junction station for the branch line to St Ives. It is also a convenient location, in the spring and summer months, to photograph the sleeper train from Paddington to Penzance which, at the date this picture was taken, departed from the capital at 23.59, arriving at Penzance at 08.37. At around 8.20 a.m. on the morning of 5 April 1988, the Paddington–Penzance sleeper train approaches St Erth station with Class 47/4 No 47458 in charge. St Erth is also famous for its large dairy and creamery, and on the left hand side can be seen some of its workers heading towards the creamery, which is just out of sight. The GWR signal box and signal complete this early morning scene.

Christina Siviter

As I write this, the Class 101 DMUs have just been withdrawn from service. They were first introduced in 1956, and built by Metropolitan Cammell.

No 51181 of that Class leaves St Erth on 5 May 1988 with the 17.14 train to St Ives, albeit a few minutes late because of the late running 15.20 Plymouth to Penzance train.

The St Ives branch swings away to the left, and in front of the train is the signal box seen in the previous picture. On the right hand side is a fine example of a GWR bracket signal.

Note that the train is leaving from the branch platform.

Roger Siviter

The last two miles of the five and a half miles between St Erth and Penzance, the line hugs the coastline of Mounts Bay, before arriving at Penzance, 162 miles from the start of our journey at the Somerset county town of Taunton.

Class 47/4 No 47614 is nicely framed by the famous Penzance station wall as it reverses out of the station with an ECS train on the morning of 30 August 1984. Above the rear of the train can be seen the roof of the station signal box.

Christina Siviter

Our final picture is slightly out of sequence, but for obvious reasons. Sadly, the Travelling Post Office (TPO) trains finished on the 9/10 January 2004. So I thought it appropriate that this last scene should show the 19.27 Penzance to Bristol TPO as it leaves Penzance and approaches Long Rock on 5 May 1988, hauled by Class 50 No 50036 *Victorious*.   *Roger Siviter*